24
24
24
24
24
24
24
24

BAM!
PAPP!

THE BUMPER BOOK OF BLACKBOARD BLUNDERS

THE BUMPER BOOK OF BLACKBOARD BLUNDERS

First published in 2009

Some text provided by Chris Stone

An Hachette UK Company
www.hachette.co.uk

Summersdale Publishers Ltd
Part of Octopus Publishing Group Limited
Carmelite House
50 Victoria Embankment
LONDON
EC4Y 0DZ

www.summersdale.com

Printed and bound in Poland

ISBN: 978-1-78685-543-5

We spend two weeks in grease every year

THE BUMPER BOOK OF BLACKBOARD BLUNDERS

You can get an electric shock from a python and be killed

RICHARD BENSON

summersdale

TO ....

FROM ....

CONTENTS

INTRODUCTION

Kids are notorious for saying the funniest things, but their writing offers gems of equal hilarity. The riotous mistakes that can emerge when children put pen to paper in an effort to express themselves would put an experienced wordsmith to shame and bring down the house in a comedy show. Yet the beauty of these errors – especially those which turn out to be nothing short of profane – is that their perpetrators are blissfully unaware of the blunder they've just made.

Sometimes the mistake, however funny, has the makings of a truly profound statement. Take, for example, the earnest and oddly accurate assertion that 'We have to look after the sky. Polution can spoil it and so can spraying too many arsols.' Others, however, are just plain silly. It is difficult to imagine how the following situation would come about: 'I dident get to sleep mutch because next doors dog was baking all night.'

So enjoy these fine examples of children's writing; you are sure to find plenty in this book to laugh about.

You've been warmed!

I ♡ SCHOOL

Mrs. Pearson said I could stay in at playtime and help her sick up some pictures on the wall.

The headteacher likes to snivel around on a black chair in his office

My teacher said I was very epidemically bright. I was prowed!

The school hell is being painted so we had assembly in our classroom.

If you are really naughty you get exploded from School

We weighed the school rabbi today, it was 2 killer grams. When he becomes four killer grams we haf to put him on a diet.

In the playground we play doctors and nurses but I got told off. I got told off because Henry had a sore throat and I put a stick on his tunge to see inside. The stick was from a tree.

The teacher in deception class looked across the room and shouted 'slop that at once!' That was a surprise.

I am verry verry sorry. It is wrong to keep giving massages to my friends when I should be listening to the teacher. I will not do it again.

When PC Handley visited he had a helmet and a smart white shit.

When Rob brought his Action Man into school it was constipated because we're not allowed toys in school.

I like to stay in at break because there are lots of birds twatting everywhere. I don't like birds.

THE TEACHER LOOKED AT MARK AND GROWLED, 'I EXPOSE YOU THINK THAT'S CLEVER!'

Once there was a dog in the playground and we went to smoke it but the dinner lady told us to keep away.

It is a hard job to be the ref but there has to be a ref if you want fore play.

We was playing football and we fell out and we started to have a fit. It was not a bad fit but the teacher tolled us of.

When we did the coin game I was the looker and Mark was the tosser.

Yesterday, Bert asked if he could burrow my football shorts at break time.

My favourite game at playtime is stock in the mud and playing with the dope. I can use a skipping dope on my own.

Inere are LOTS of birds in the school garden. The other day I saw some tits and a chaffage. The chaffage was pink and grey.

I found a spare seal so I quickly sat on it

Teacher said I couldn't do PE becqu̇se I hadn't brot my pimps.

When we do PE, Billy is good at four wood rolls

WE HAVE A SPINACH GIRL COMING TO STAY. I WON'T KNOW WHAT TO SAY TO HER THOUGH BECAUSE I DON'T SPEAK SPINACH.

We made a leaving card for Mrs. Bow. because She is being retarded at the end of term.

When I finish junior school I go to comprehending school.

My skool unicorn is blue trousers and a purple coat.

It used to be Mummy who took me to school, but now we have a big new bust that takes us.

Miss Ancliffe always tells us to shit the door behind us.

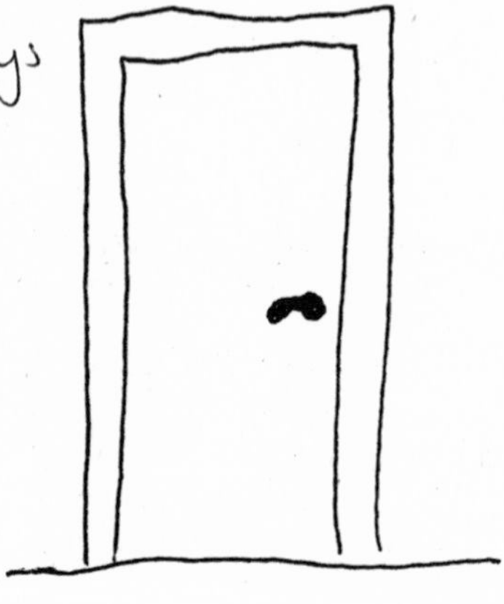

I've been told I can take violence lessons in my music class, except I'd rather play the piano.

My class saw French people when we went on the you're a star.

i'm very bendy and I can do the spits.

Mum is happy becawse the school she picked for me is in the catching area.

Sometimes the teachers go to school and the boys and girls play at home. That is called incest days.

Archie got exuded. He put a sink bomb in the girls toilets

I brought tins of food for the oldery people when it is the Hardest Festival.

Mr. Brown walked into the room and sat on his favourite choir.

Dad says it's not about the whining, its about the taking part

Jimmy was threatened with extinction by Mr Moss for being so naughty.

On Tuesday the fire alarm bell rang and the teachers said resemble in the car park.

Mummy says I've got a good voice and I should sign in the choir.

When the Head Master comes in we stand behind our decks and say Good Moaning.

I want to ride a bike to school but I'm worried my feet will get dizzy.

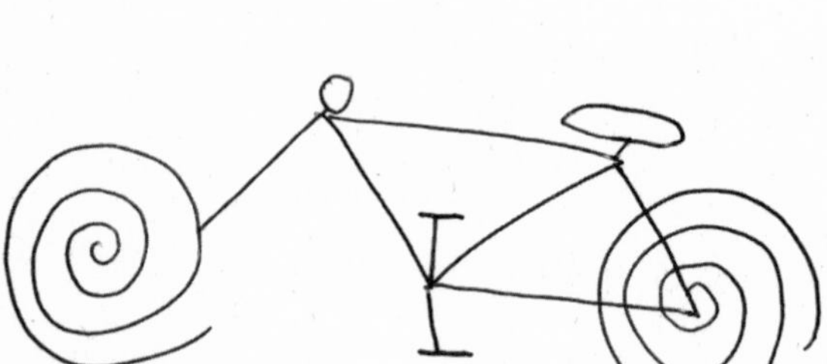

I came home early today cos there were no extra circular activists.

Callum and me keep missing the bus. The teacher says we need to be more punctural.

Muck excams are the practice for the real ones.

Me and my best friend Ellie want to learn to speak a forein languid.

Before I went to big school
I went to the local primal school.

If you don't do werk, you have to
face the quenchy quenchies.

Mr Smith was sick on friday so we had a supple teacher instead.

In the dining room we ate pizza, chips and beans and for desert it was Arctic Role.

I don't pronounce words very well and I might have to have electrocution lessons.

CREATIVE WRITING

YOU HAVE TO BOO EARLY FOR THE SCHOOL PLAY.

I luv J.K. Rolling, She is my heroin.

When you write a story you should do a daft copy first.

If you dont want to use a full stop you can use an exsitement mark instead!

"You are under a rest and you will be remembered in custard for the night," said the policeman. He wasnt expecting that!

In the next part of the story, the judge condomned the prisoner to death

The pilot was about to crash the plane. The moment he saw his wig come off and fall to the ground he knew there was no chance of survival.

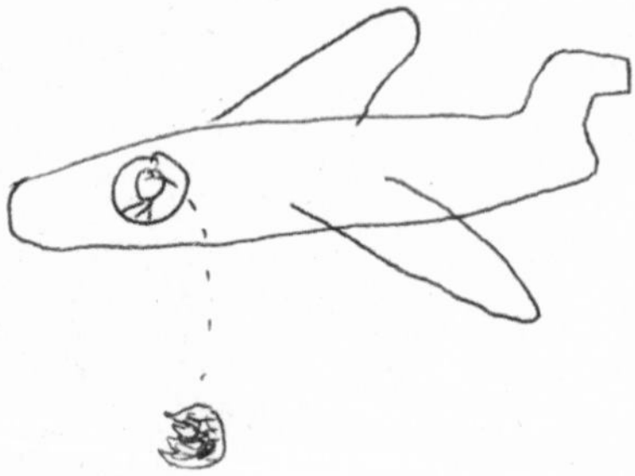

'And now' declared Mr. Scarlett-Jones 'I shall read your uncle's last will and testicle.'

Robert was in a very bad crash and he has not wocken up from it. I think he is in a cromer.

Time seemed to be standing still. Nothing was happening and I was getting scarred. I looked again at my cock. It hadn't moved since I last looked at it.

There was an accident on our road last night and a man was badly enjoyed.

As he stepped outside he gave a quick nob of his head and everybody knew what he meant.

THE WHISTLE SOUNDED AND SMOKE PAWED OUT FROM THE SHIP'S FLANNEL

The magician tapped on his majik box and said 'abracadabra' and then varnished under the table.

'Look at your hands!' said Mrs. Grumble. 'I don't know where you've been but they're as black as the arse of spades!'

The driver flashed at me so I decided to cross the road

Some of the houses were so big that the owners turned them into flats so they could make lots of money from their todgers.

When my big sister played Goldilocks
I was aloud in the concert too.
I just had to be a little bare.

There was a very thick frog on the roads
last night and it maid a car crash
into a bus.

Once there was a forest
bear
He had green nose hair,
That's quite rare,
So Dad attacked him.

Dracula was a famous umpire, he went round bating people.

My favrit book is The Twats by Rold Dahl.

My sister loves the books about Whinny the Poo the best.

At big school my oldest sister Sarah is reading Withering Tights. Its written by a famous Brummy.

In the olden days Shakspeer wrote plays such as Romeo and Julian.

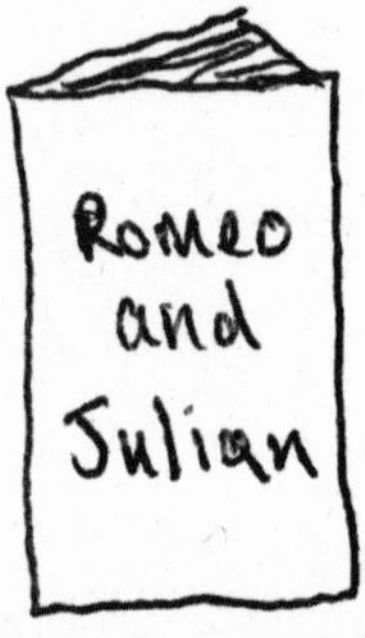

ART AND MUSIC

I'm good at sewing. I will be able to run up curtains soon

I LOVE DRAWING AND PAINTING SO MY FAVOURITE SUBJECT IS ARS

Today I painted an octopuss with big eyes and eight purple testicles

My dad's best ever movie is raging balls.

Mums favourite film is When Hairy Met Sally.

Uncle Pete told me off in the cinema cos I was running in the ale.

I had a babysitter when mum and dad went to the theatre in Dreary Lane.

When we went to London we went to Madam 2 swords.

Our class went to watch a play outdoors in an ample theatre.

Grandad is older than 65 so he got a cheap ticket to the museum called a concussion.

In last years christmas play Linzi played the main prat. I played one of the smaller prats and I would like to have a bigger prat next year.

. . . and at the end of the show we all sing away in a manager.

In art we are learning about abstract artists like mark rothko and jackson pillock.

When I grow up I want to be a artist so I can pant all the time.

In France their are some very famous paintings like Moaning Lisa

My favourite colour is punk

When my family go to the cinema I like to eat poopcorn.

I like musical instruments I've asked Farther Cristmas for a sexaphone

Grandad likes classical music. I think its boring but he likes the sympathies.

Today I learned there is an arte galley in Paris called The Loo.

Pistachio is famous for a painting about gurning.

Auntie Ann plays the flute and reads shit music.

I like to play percussion my favourite is when I shake the tangerine or when I use my dong on the triangle.

We went to the natural history museum in London and saw lots of insex.

I love Ariana Grande
but mum says she
prefers the spliced girls.

Vincent van cough
painted sunflowers.

Mum got a carry OK machine for dads 50th birthday party

If you got to the theatre and people sing alot thats the oprah

Granddad has an old thing called a record player for his final records

GEOGRAPHY

In the middle of London
towering over the River Tems
is an enormous building
called Big Ben. It is
probably the biggest
cock in the world.

They are
trying to close the
pubic footpath behind
our house.

The world has got two hemisfears, one at the top and one in the bottom.

If a volcano erupts its really really hot and lots of lather comes out of it.

The north pole is so cold that the people that live there have to live sum wear else.

You use the 24 hour clock in summer because it stays light longer.

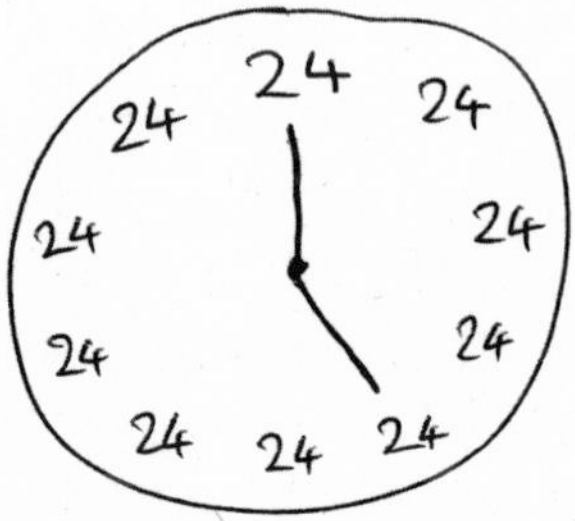

The closest town to France is Dover. You can get to France on a train or you can go on a fairy.

In geography we learned that countries with sea round them are islands and ones without sea are incontinent.

They used to think the earth was fat but it is really round. It is shaped like a spear.

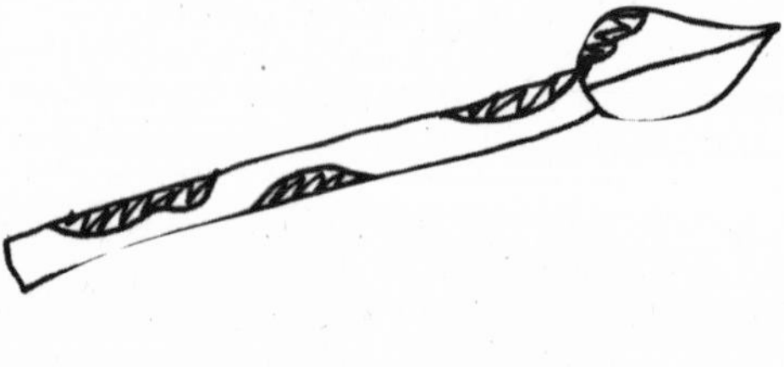

In Scandinavia, the Danish people come from Denmark, the Norwegians come from Norway and the Lapdancers came from Lapland.

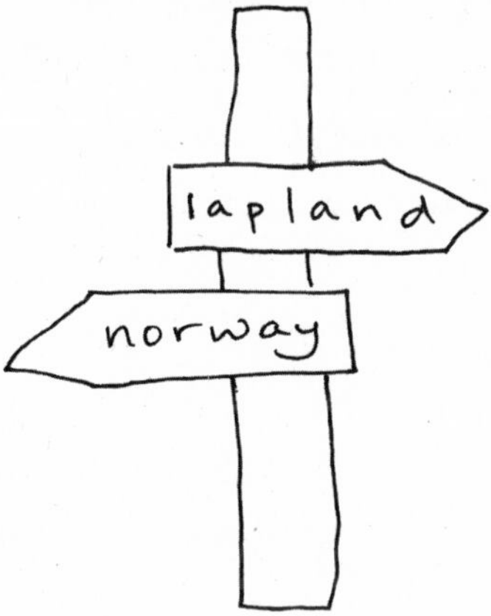

A FLAT MOP OF THE WORLD IS AN ATLESS. A ROUND MOP IS A GLOB. GLOBS ARE MORE INTRESTING.

I feel sorry for the children of Africa. They're starving to death. They only have a little groin to eat. I would not like to eat groin.

When theres lots of rain sometimes cliffs can road into the sea.

The Specific Ocean is the big sea on the left next to America.

A Ship's window is called a pothole.

On the globe there are lines of platitude and longitude.

Our school whent on a trip to some big rocks called Stone Hedge.

The oldest pyramids are the ones in geezer

The president of Russia lives in a big place in Moscow called the Gremlin.

The second largest river in the world is the Amazing River.

Europe is one of the world's seven incontinents.

Mount Everest has the biggest peek in the world.

In the UK the time is called Grenich mene time.

There are lots of different types of clods. There is one called Sirus and one called Status.

Today Mr Walls got me and Sam to plot a grid rererence on the map.

When a big river turns into more rivers there are tributes

In Paris our school went in the Eyeful Tower

Some people who have always lived in a particular place are in dijerness.

In Australia the Aborigines live in Air Rock.

One of the BIG mountans you can walk up is kill a man Jiro.

Waterfalls are awesome. One day I would like to go to Viagra falls which is the biggest in the world.

There are lots of plates in the ground called tonic plates. When they move around they cause earthquakes.

Our school trip was to see the caves at the Cheddar George.

Next term were going orienteering to lean about using accomplice.

Billy and me tried to find the woods near my house on the ordinary survey map.

We learnt about Africa in geography class, I would like to see the wild breasts roaming the plane.

THERE ARE LOTS OF CARNIVOROUS FORESTS IN SCOTLAND. AND IN THE FORESTS YOU CAN SEE DEARS AND SLAGS.

MATHS

I need to work hard on my maths so I will be god at it.

We drew a giraf to show how many trafics went passed the school.

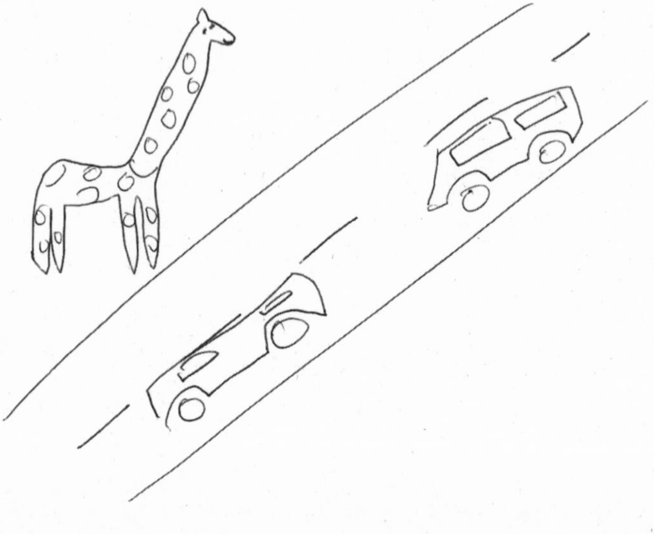

Frackchens are like harvs garters and tirds.

When I go to big school I will learn maths like algenia. My brother does algenia and he always needs to find x.

Mr Collins said my homework was good but the answers were not right because the decibel point was in the wrong place.

I would like to be an accountant but you have to know a lot about moths.

TWO HALVES MAKE A WHALE

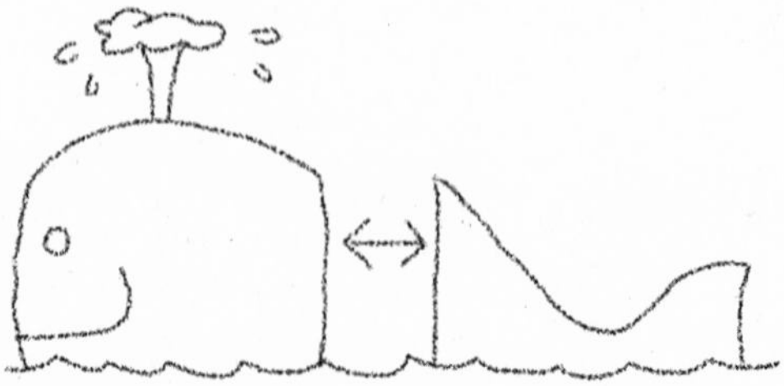

The total is when you add up all the numbers. A remainder is an animal that pulls santa on his slay.

When two things are the same they have cemetery.

Miles are smaller than killer meters.

If it is less than
90 degrees it is a
cute angel.

The most popular crisps
were salt and vinegar
and the least popular
were ready slated.

Circumstance is all the way
round the circle to the start
again.

The diane meter is the circle measure from one side across to the other end.

If you guess but you dont guess high enough yu undress to mate.

MY CONCLUSION FROM THE SURVEY IS THAT PEOPLE WHO DON'T HAVE CARS DON'T DRIVE TO WORK.

My favourite teacher is Mr. Bronwen. He is the meth teacher. I love doing meth with him.

Alfies big brother does maths about pie fagorus.

The bit from the end of the Circle to the middle bit is a radio.

In olden times when nanna and grandad were young they had money called fartlings and stroppy bits.

If we don't know the answer the teacher lets us use a calibrator.

A shape that has 6 sides is called a heptathlete

The difference between 3 and 1 is that 3 is a curly shape and 1 is straight.

The numbers that are the same that you multiply together are common factories.

Maths doesn't ever stop. The numbers keep on going untill infidgety.

1,000,000,000,000,000,
000,000,000,000,000,
000,000,000,000,000,
000,000,000,000,000,

If you way something it can be in killergrans, or in pounds and ounces.

Last week in maths we looked at angles and today we will be doing purple dickular lines.

2 and 3 and 5 are examples of primal numbers.

I like aiding and subtracting the best.

Mr Tillis got our class to work out the degrees in an angle with a tractor.

Angels that are inbetween 90 and 180 degrees are obese.

I wanted to learn about big numbers more than a hundred but the teacher said its not on the silly bus.

things that are not flat
have three mentions.

2 and 4 are even
numbers and 1 and
3 are strange.

SCIENCE

One of the most important farces is the farce that pulls things down to the ground. This farce is called gravy.

when me and Sarah rubbed two materials together it created fiction.

Today our teecher tort us about the new Hardon Collider. when its turned on it could corse a big bang.

when me and Sarah rubbed two materials together it created fiction.

You can get an electric shock from a python and be killed.

Helicopters are cleverer than planes. Not only can they fly through the air they can also hoover.

Smog is a kind of dirty fog. It is made by plution. In some cantrys they have smog every day and pepol even have to wear masks to stop it from herting them.

Our Solar System is made of a sun, nine plants, lots of moons and balls of fire which fly around inside the system and can cause damage. These are called hemaroids.

Computers have made our lives easier. But sometimes do not. They often break down and we get sperm-mail.

YOU'VE GOT MAIL!

We can all see things because we have a septic nerve that joins our eyes to our brians.

The sun rises in the east and sets in the west. This is why it's hotter in the east.

If there are alans out in space I would like for them to come to earth and say hello. Or whatever you say if you are an alan.

the biggest boner in the
human body is in your thigh.

People stay on the
ground and don't
float up to the
sky because of
grabitational pull.

IN ELECTRIC PLUGS THERE'S AN EARTH WIRE A NEUTRAL WIRE AND AN ALIVE WIRE.

Our science lesson was all about voles and currants.

Really great scientists can do things like spit atoms.

All materials in the worlds is either solid, gas or a quid.

When the earth spins it does not stand up straight. It spins on its axe.

I want to meet a
little green man in space or
another person who are
extra testical life.

Mr Walbert told us that nuclear is
dangerous and radiators that
come out of it have half lives.

When we do our science homework we
always have to write it like this:
Apparatus, method results, collusion.

Today science was really yukky.
The teacher digested a toad.

Saturn is one of the planets in
the solar cistern.

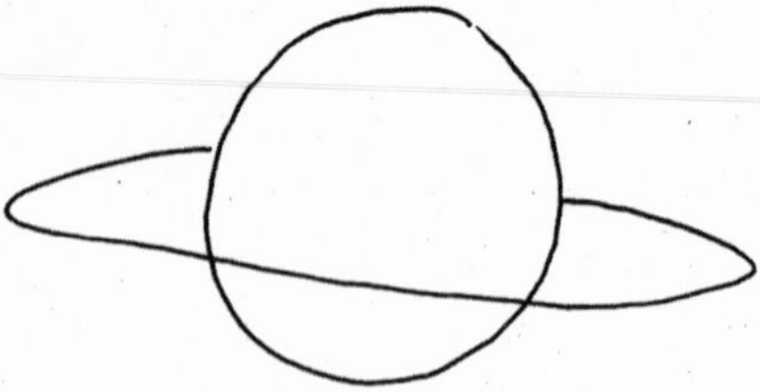

The patriotic Table is a big list of all
the elements in science.

I was a bit scared so the teacher helped me to light the bum tum burner

Our class does lots of experiments in the science laratories

God liked Saturn because he put a ring on it.

ALL PROPER SCIENTISTS HAVE WHITE GHOSTS.

Humans bread out carbon monoxide and plants bread it in

Everyone has big intesticles and small intesticles to help their food go down.

In biology we learn about all the different prats in the human body

Oxygen is the air that keeps all the people breeding all day.

If you don't aspire then you won't breed properly

HISTORY

My favourite subject is history. I like looking into the post to see what I can find.

If you had no money in the 1930s you could get some by going to the porn shop. The man at the porn shop had 3 balls hanging over his entrance.

King Richard the third extinguished himself in battle.

On Army's stis day we have to wear puppies pinned on our jumpers.

Sir Walter Raleigh circumcised the world
with his massive chipper

Then Joan of Ark met her end.
She was burned as a steak.

We buy poopies and wear them
all week. On poopy day we all
go quiet and think about dead
people.

In the olden days cars were not ~~alloued~~ aloud to go fast. The first cars had to follow a man with a fag in his hand.

For the first time in history people could have mashines to help them with their work at home. You could have a frig in your kichen.

If you did something brave in the war you might get a meddle.

The Suek Canal was important because people didn't have to make the boats go round the other way

Dad did a family tree to find out about our aunt sisters.

Florence Nitingale was known as the lady with the lump.

... and in the 1970s there was a law that said there must be sexy quality for women.

In wartime children who lived in big cities had to be evaporated because it was safer in the country.

People who came from Normandy in middle age were called Norman

In the oldern days
the streets were very
bumpy because they
were full of cobblers.

Sometimes in the war
they take prisners
and keep them as
ostriges until the
war is over. Some
prisners end up in
consterpation camps.

The sufrajets complaned for voles for women.

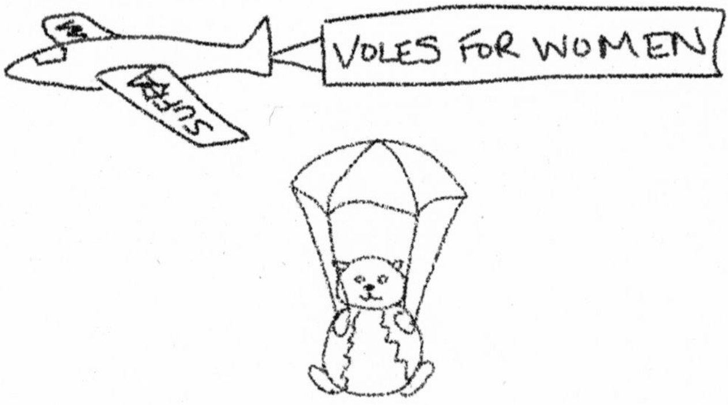

There are two houses of parliament in our country. The main one is the house of comons. The other is the house of lards.

Captain Cok was a famous exploder.
He soiled the seas in his soiling ship.

In the field near our house they
think they have found the remains
of a Roman fart.

I had travelled back in time to the war. I tried to buy a drink but I only had new money on me and it was going to cost me a shilling. What could I do?

The sultanas had wifes and also porcupines.

The easter game of egg rolling started in debenhams and cornwall.

Groucho Marx invented communalism
which is where everybody
shares all there things.

In the old times the pheasants had to
do all the work for the lords of
the manner.

Dico dansing started when my mum was young. Before that there was lots of other danse fashons. In the 1920s there were girls called floppers

THE ANCENT EGIPTIANS WROTE IN HYDROLICS.

Napoleon expired in 1821.

Greek Gods. The three gods in my project are the King of the gods – Zeus, the messenger of the gods – Hermes, and the god of war – Arse.

Today we learned about US president ronald ray gun.

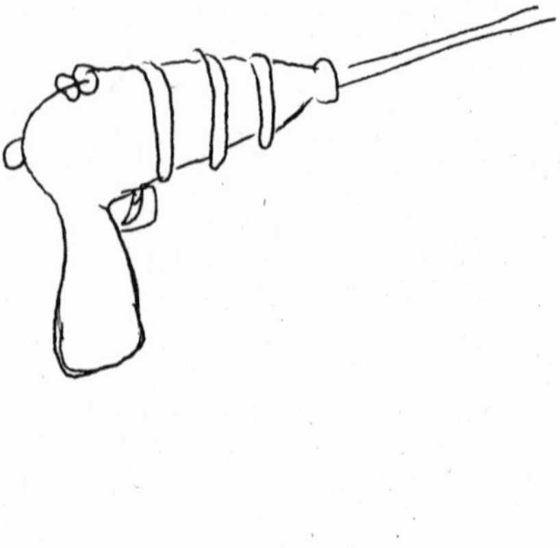

Some of the USA presidents like JFK got assimilated.

Alexander the Grate was in charge before the time of Jesus

William the conker won the Battle of Hastings.

When slaves were freed in South Africa it was called a party.

The Romans built aqua ducks and straight roads.

In Russia and France and some other places there were revulsions.

When Japan bombed Paul Harbor the USA retaliated.

Some things Nostrodamoose said were poetic but most of them was lies.

In the really olden times when two men were angry with each other they got up mega early in the morning and had a jewel.

The most impotent people in ancient Egypt were the pharoahs.

George Washington chopped up a cheery tree and told his dad which was nice

Christopher Columbia went in a boat to find the united Americans on a cauliflower.

Back in the evil period people didn't wash or have proper toilets

Lots of soldiers died during the Thirst World War and we remember them every year

When lots of people who live in the same country fight each other its called a Cyril War.

Queen Victoria wore black clothes
and rained for ages

Adolf Hitter was really
bad. He killed the chews
and no one liked him
apart from his mum.

In the seventeenth cemetery there was a big fire in london

England didnt have a king when the cavaliers were fighting Oliver Crumwell and the bigheads

WHAT I DID ON MY HOLIDAYS...

On our activity
holiday Dad wanted
to ride the hores
but mum said they
were too ekspensive.

We spend two weeks
in grease every year

My uncle Steve took my cusins to Blackpool to see the aluminashons. We went to Blackpool as well but we went to see the lights.

WE NEARLY RAN OVER A PEASANT IN THE WEEKEND. IT RAN OUT FROM A FRAMYARD.

This holiday we got some slobs to make a patio in the back garden.

Some of the biggest fish my dad had caught are from our holidays. He has caught pikes and craps.

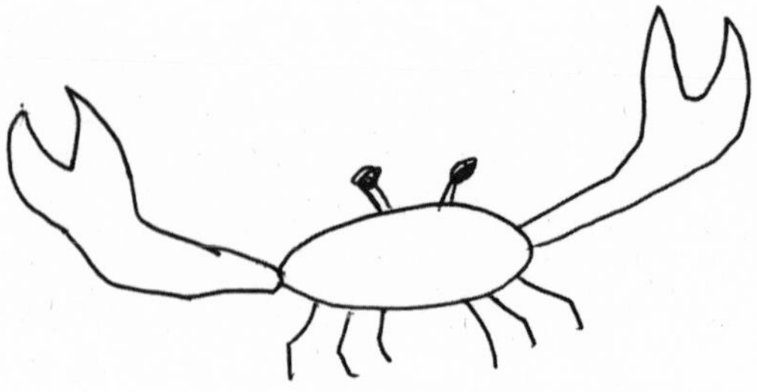

When we were in Scotland we used to go into the woods for a walk. Dad liked to see how many beers he could see.

When it gets near crismas I get choelat penis. I get one evry morning.

Santa carries all the toys in a big sock on his back.

I went to Kenya for my holidays. I went not to have a safari adventure but a family one. We went because all my family lives there... Except my mum, dad, my brother, me and my sister.

It was peek season when we went on holiday to the beach. There were ladles in bikinis everywhere.

Last Christmas I heard Santa putting the presents in our living room. He nocked over something and swared like daddy.

In the winter we went to lapland
and we had a ride on a sled
with some hussies.

Dad said wait with
mum while he got
the suitcases off
the baggage
caramel.

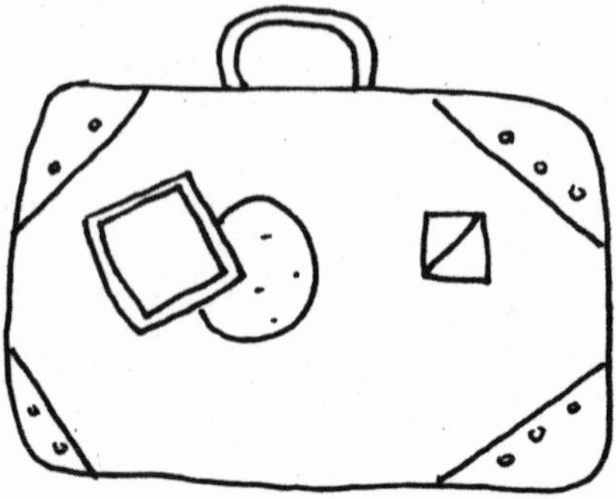

When the fire alarm went off in the hotel everyone had to evaporate.

I liked the aeroplane. The air stewart give me I scream

For my holidays I went to Euroland and met Snow Wipe and Sleeping Booty. I met Mickey Mouse. he is a real mouse.

Me and my brother got all the cushions and we made a massive fart.

Uncle pat was grumpy at the hotel. He said the drinks were two expensive and theres no hippy hour.

Mum and aunt bella did the water arabics in the pool every morning.

My best friend Sean went to a really hot place in the summer. I can't remember what its called but he said it's near the Meditation Sea.

When we go to Spain we live next to the sandy bitch.

Dad says we are having a staycation this year. I think he's driving us to central parts.

Breakfast was boring. It was just cheese and ham really. Mum said it was an incontinent one.

Me and my cousins and the mums and dads are living in a big villain in the holidays.

We went to the fun fair on our holidays and played hook a duck. My mum is the best hooker.

Dad pitched the tent but mum told him off because he left the ground sheep at home.

My family goes to a campsite and stays in a mobile home.

It was really hot in eejit and I liked it when we rode the camels.

Sally heard mum and dad Say we a renting a parchment for a fortnight.

It was super cool when I zoomed in the waves in an unflappable dingy.

Aunty Debbie went to the Far East
n Winter time and had tie messages.

christmas is my favorit time of year. I love
Satan. I wish Satan was my dad.

We almost missed our plane when the taxi took us to the wrong terminator

When Im older dad says I should go youth travelling like he did

I like going in the sea in the summer. I wanted to do windsuffering but mum says im too little

The rich people in our street go to Cany beans for two hole weeks.

Mum said we could eat and drink whatever we liked at the hotel because it was all intrusive

Nan and Granddad couldn't go on holiday.
There was a hurrycan and their hotel fell over.

In florida I got my
photo taken with
Mikey Moose.

The Captin said he was flying the plane
at a really high attitude.

RELIGIOUS STUDIES

Dear God, my wish is
that there would be
pis all over the world.
Make the wars end
and pipol live in pis
all their lives...

If you marry two people you are a
pigamist, but morons are allowed to
do this.

Jesus died cross, he had bleeding feet and he was stoned.

The church near my hous is three hundred years away, we go there on wholly days and Sindays.

I did a cak stall for charity, i sold all my caks. The Cristian charity was a non-prophet organisation.

A mosque is a sort of church. The main difference is that its roof is doomed.

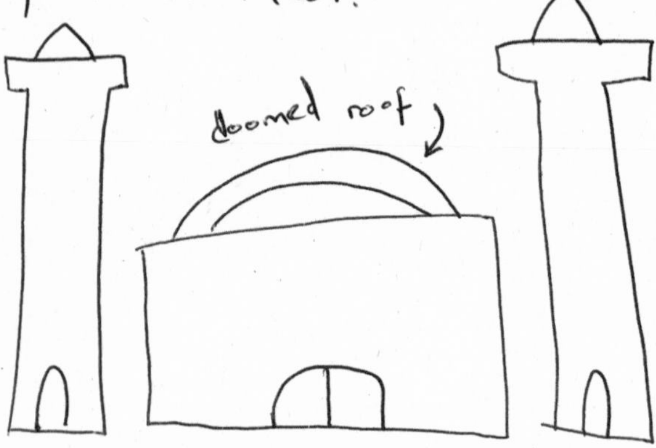

Lustily Mary and Josef
whent to the final hotel.
They didnent find a room
So they went to a Stable.

Jesuses dad was josef.
He was a crapinter.

In jewish churches they do not have vikers. In sted they have rabbits.

IF A CATHOLIC PERSON TELLS LIES ITS OK BECAUSE THEY CAN GO TO A CONVENTIONAL AND SAY SORRY.

Oh come let us ignore him
Oh come let us ignore him
Oh come let us ignore him
Price that lawn.

Adam was lonely so he
made Eve out of a
apple tree.

The most famous of the ten commendments is thou shalt not comment on a duckery.

Monks are men who give their life to God and many nuns. They live in a monstery.

God looks after us when we are sleeping because he has a special key to let himself in.

I asked my mum why we said old men at the end of prayers at skool. I don't know any old men apart from my grandpa.

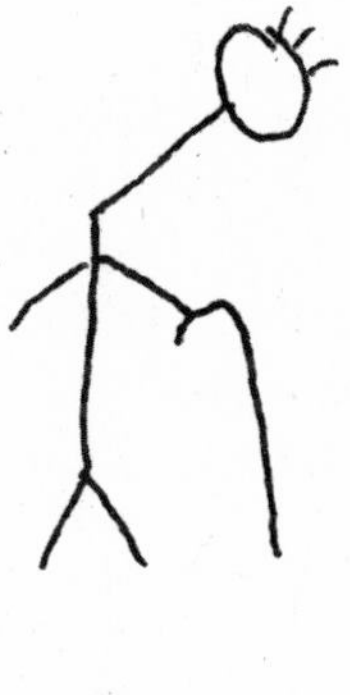

All over the world there are different religions. The people dress diffrent and do diffrent things but one thing is the same. They worship a gog.

Mary and Joseph had to go to Bethlehem on a donkey because everyone els had taken all the taxis.

Jesus had twelve decibels who helped people hear his teachings.

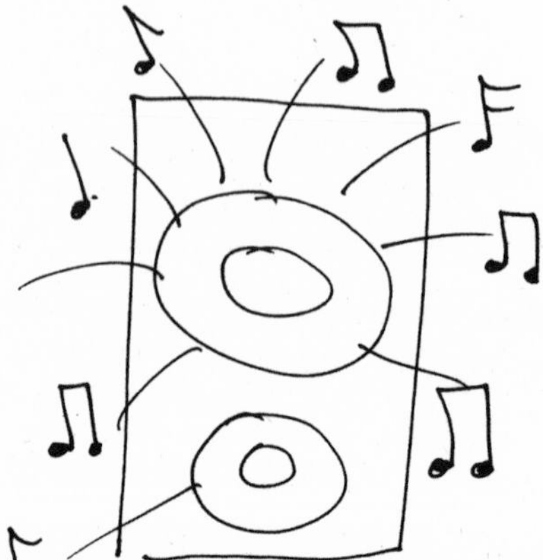

Harry was Joseph in the Naivety Play.

Angels don't eat but they drink milk from holy cows.

My farourit part of church is when we go home at the end.

Our father, who art in heaven, Harold is his name... And lead us not into temptation, but deliver us some email.

MY AUNT GOES TO CHURCH EVERY SUNDAY AND PREYS ABOUT THE HOLY GOATS.

In the bible Moses partied the Sea of Gallilee.

When Chris was put on the cross at Easter it was really bad. It was crucial fiction and he didnt have any eggs.

Granny says be a good girl because God nose everything.

At church the priest told everyone God is ominous.

The stories Jesus told that teach us lessons are probables.

Jesus said I cum in pies. But not everyone believed him.

Jesus was born because Mary had an immaculate contraption

Samsung was a big strong man with long hair but Delia cut it off and Samsung lost all its power.

When you are 100
and you might die
you can go to heaven
or down at heel.

God created Adam and Ebay.

"Little Donkey, Little Donkey, on
a crusty road..."

A eightiest is someone who doesn't believe in God.

In the nativity play I was a shepard. I had to wash my flock with a stick in my hand.

Milly and Jane said that their parents are Roman Catholic, so I told them that our family are all prostitutes.

"Here's the church,
here's the staples,
open the doors,
here's all the peoples!"

Today I learned about doughnut and the whale in Sunday school. Doughnut was eaten by the whale because he'd been a bad doughnut.

God spoke to me one night. He said 'Rmmrrm!' But it might have been a lawn mower.

The three wise men brought Gold, franking sense and more.

I asked mum whose that man with the white hair on the box of oats. She said it was to do with religion and he was quackes.

A carnation is all about life after death.

In the bible, Joan was swallowed by a big Wail. That wasn't very nice.

The leader of the England Church is the arch bishop of cadbury.

The vicar was wearing a black shirt and a white strip around his neck. Dad said it was a dog caller.

If you stop in the road to help a person whose hurt themself you are a good summertime.

NATURAL HISTORY

I herd the owl say twat-to-woo in my bed. My mum said it was a tawny owl.

I love the deers. Particularly the slags that fight with theeir anklers.

Every living thing is an orgasm. From the smallest cell to a whole mammal, there are orgasms everywhere.

In Australia they have small Kangaroos as well. They are called wallies

Baby cows are carves and
baby bulls are bollocks.

My hobby is insest. I lern about all kinds of insest from a book I bort at the bring and bye sale. I speshly like aunts.

Elephants love to eat penis.
But not ones with salt on them.

Ostralia is famos for its speshal animals like kangeroos, coia bears and cookerbuggers. You cant get these anywer els.

The best place to put tropical pants is somewhere warm and damp, where they can live happily.

I lik to pik up smells on the beach and keep them in my room.

That is the end of my project on porkypines. My next one will be about armydildos.

We have to look after the Sky. Polution can spoil it and so Can spraying too many arsols.

Crabs can hurt sometimes because they have princes that give a nasty nip.

Crap rotation is what farmers do when they have grown some crap in a field for a long time

Fax hunting is cruel. Faxes can be a bit of a newsance at times, but it is still wrong to get dogs to rip the poor little fax to shreds. I think fax hunting should be made ~~illegal~~. illigitimate.

Crabs and creatures like them all belong to a family of crushed asians.

A bottomist is a person who works with plants.

Today I lernt about lemons. Lemons jump off cliffs to their deaths. I would not want to be a lemon.

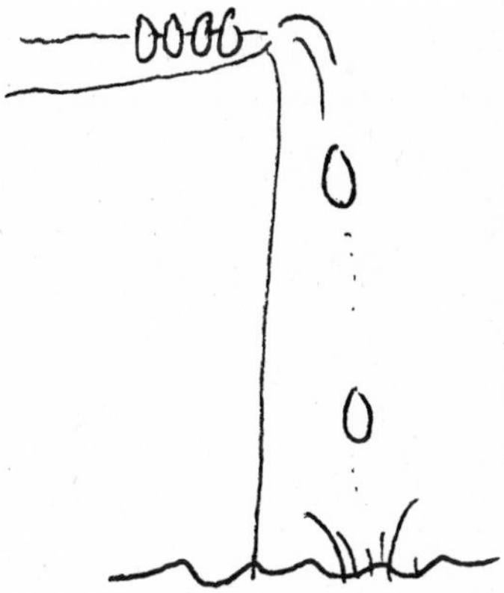

I saw a hedgehog today and it had pickles all over it.

I want to see a gruffalo. I think it looks a bit like a willy mammoth.

The biggest jungle in the hole wide world is in the amazing basin.

I went to the zoo with my class. My favourite animal was a fricken elephant.

A dolphin breathes through its bottom on the top of its face.

Mum put bird seed out for the robbing red best when it was snay.

The jungles of Africa are very dangerous for the people who explore them. There must be hundreds of people who have been maulled to death by a tiger or lino.

. . . and there are monkeys
with red bottoms called
buffoons. . .

owls and badgers sleep
in the morning time but are
awake at night because
they are notorious.

I fed the baby ghost some hay at the farm. It was a kid.

Trees where all their leaves fall out are assiduous

All the animals that have bones are verticals and the other ones are inverticals

When I was playing with Darren I put my hand in stinking nettles and it hurt.

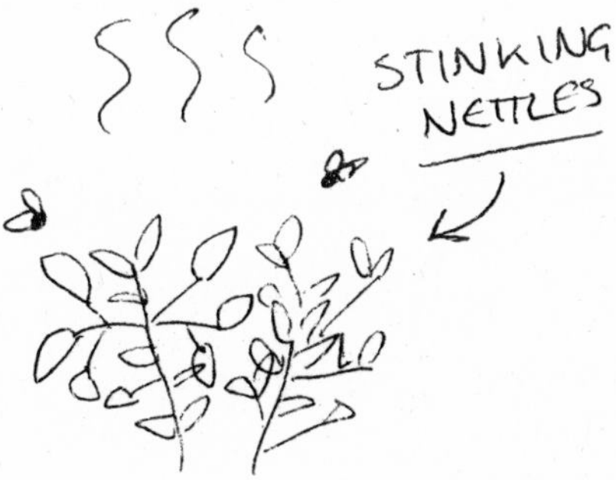

Male sheep are rams and lady sheep are you.

Mum took me to the garden centre. She bought hydrators and pianos.

OUR TORTUS LIVES IN THE SHED IN THE WINTER. ITS HIDERNATING.

Moles and rabbits are kinds of borrowing animals

Id like to see elephants if I
can go to africa on suffery.

Purposes live in the sea
and are a bit like dolpins

Sea enemies are plants that sit on a rock and wobble about in the water.

our class went to cue gardens to visit the plants and I see why it was called that because there was a big cue to get in.

If people chop all the trees down
there will be no jingles left.

The teacher told us frogs
and toads are fibbers

Its mean to keep birds in little
Cajuns. They need to have a
big one to have room to fly
around.

DINNER TIME

Everymorning dad has a slice of dread before he goes to work.

I went for a curry and had two nuns. My dad had a burma.

Our cousins eat posh French food like cock o van.

We made panics on stove Tuesday.

When we go and see my nan she always gives us lots of nise things to eat. My mum has a current bum and I have a batenball cake.

Sparkling water is carbon dated.

The pizza we ate on Saturday had cheese and tomato sauce on. It was called margaret.

The best dinner is spagete bolonase. Its main ingredients are pasta, sause and minge meat.

All our family love sweats. I like sticky buns with icing on top but my mum is the worsed. She loves bras of chocolate. She had three chocolate bras on Friday evening last week.

Last week it was Jack's berthday. He brort a cak to school and we all had a pis. I had a pink pis.

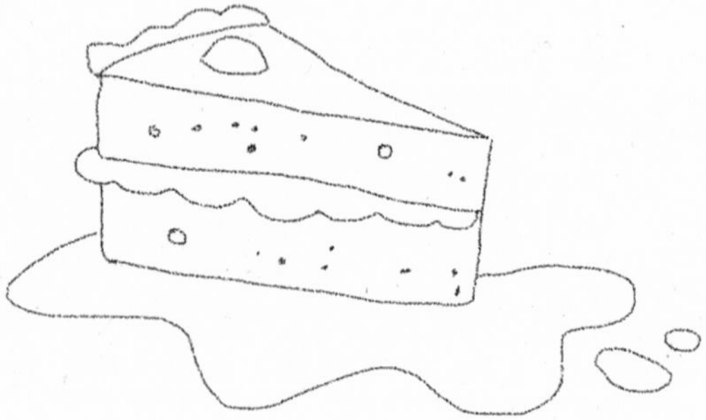

I love toucans on my soup. They're really crunchy but also a bit chewy and get stuck in my teeth.

Pancakes are like normal cakes but without any ingredients. This is why their flat.

We got our tea from the chinees last night. I love orimental food.

The teacher said my jam tarts showed
I have good canary skills

I eat shreddded wit for
breakfust and my
Sister has tost.

They couldn't fit us in for a meal at the restraint because we hadn't reversed a table.

My big sister is a vagetarian.

On speshal ocashuns and partys i am alowed coke. My dad has wiskey. He says its his favrit nipple.

You can make toste by putting the bread in a toster or by putting it under a girl until it is done.

My favourite food
is ham buggers.

At the weekend sometimes
we have hoe made cakes.

My mum is really good at
cocking the dinner.

I like jelly but I don't
like blue minge.

Susie doesnt have milk or
cheese at school because
she can't have diary.

When I lie the table
for dinner mum
says put out the
compliments like
mayonase and ketchup.

Some things are quicker to eat if
you heat them up in a microphone.

My mum's a virgin because she doesn't eat meat or butter.

When we were in france dad had a big plate of muscles. They were all slimey and disgusting.

It was mum and dad's wedding anniversary. They drank Shampoo to celebrate.

Advocates are actually a fruit because they have a stone.

it was internashional food day at school. The Mexican fat heaters were best.

I USUALLY HAVE BREAKFAST BUT TODAY I LOST MY APPLE TIGHTS.

Indian takeaway is too hot in my mouth but I had a bit of mums popperdoms and pillow rice.

Pisses of pasta with things inside it is called ravey olly.

My dad isn't very well today because of his overhang.

my favourit puddings are ice cream sunday and banana Splat.

When I went to Tillys for a playdate her mum helped us make fiery cakes.

I HAD SOUP OF THE DAY AT THE PUB. IT WAS CALLED MINESTONEY AND I LIKED THE CRETINS THAT WERE FLOATING ON THE TOP.

The butcher didn't have any nice lamb so we had mitten instead.

Christmas dinner is my favorite meal ever. My mum always cooks turkey, stuffing, roast potatoes and vegetables like carrots and parsons.

I FEEL SICK!

I went to see the docter because I kept getting crap. I woak up with the crap all down my leg yesterday and I cuddent put my foot down.

The dentist sicked a sicker on my front for being gud.

I brock my tooth and had to get a feeling from the dentist.

If you feel portly go to the nurse and docter.

I Kept filling the sock so I was not in school last Week

When you get bitten by a snack you need to drink the anecdote

The docter said I shud stay in bed for a few days cos I had blaked sins.

Safety is very impotent. My brother was unsafe on his bikaycle and he fell off and broked a bone in his back called his cockstick.

I keep getting whacks in my ear and it makes me a bit def. I think the docter will try to suck it out.

I was scarred of going to the bentist but I just felt a little prick and went to sleep.

Sometimes if you are reely reely poorly you go to a speshal ward in hospital and the ward is called insensitive care.

After I saw the school nurse I felt better, on the hole.

My brother broked his humorous bone in his arm, he had a plaster put on and a large slong.

When I am sick mum says I am portly and under the weather

When my brother had a feever he had a temperance of more than a hundred

I have to ware glasses like mum and dad. Mum says bad sight runs in the family which means its heretic.

The norse said sorry to mum because we had to wait ages and there were loads of patience.

uncle gary was too fat and then
the doctor said he had dying beetles.

When we go on holiday mum always packs
a thirst aid kit just in case someone gets
hurt or sick.

Aunt Sarah has accupuncture when a man sticks pens in her neck. It sounds painful!

I dont like staying in the hospital. Its smelly and the food is disguising

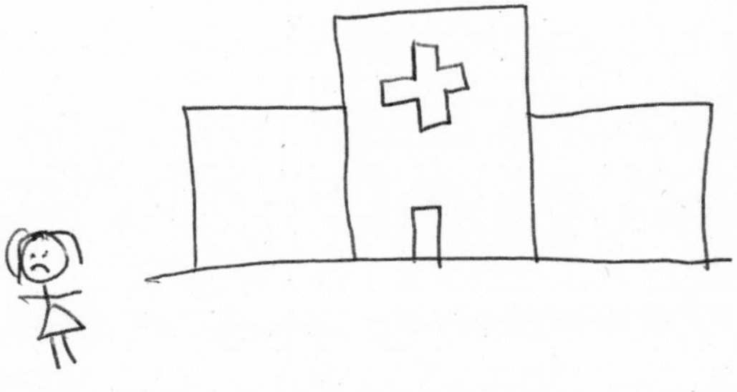

Grandad is going into a home for old people because he is incontinental.

Bellas mum doesn't like dirty things in the house. She uses anti sceptic wipes to make it cleaner.

When she gets my graines in her head mum takes asprins

The doctor let me use her periscope to hear my heartbeat.

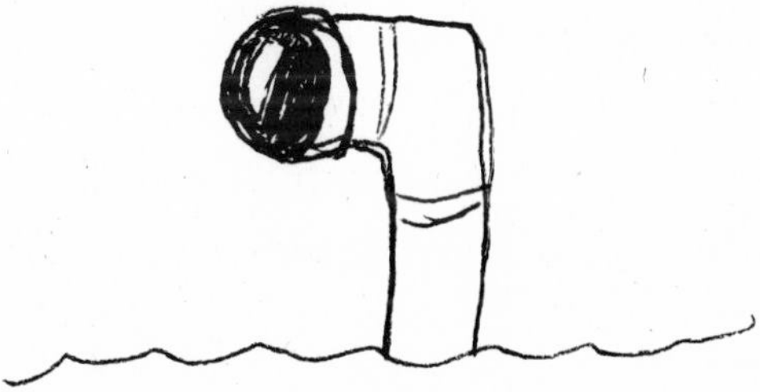

We were at the hospital
because Algie banged his
head playing football.
People was worryed he
might have a conclusion.

My baby brother got hopping cough
and he was really nosey and
I didnt sleep much.

The doctor has given me anti erotics to make me better. It tastes a bit like bananas but yucky bananas.

Gayles baby keeps crying and dribeling. She says he is teetering

My mum gives me coff sirup when I have a sure throat

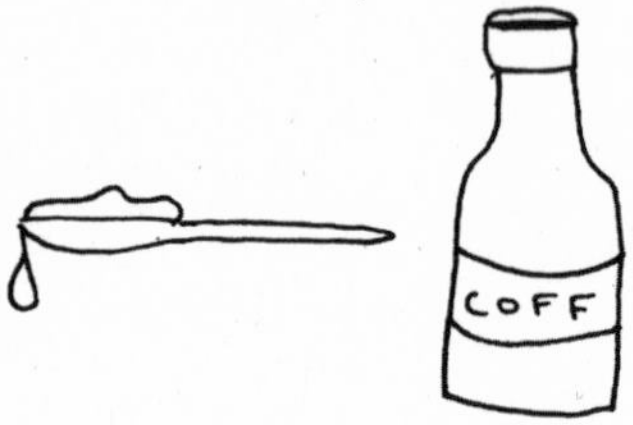

My leg was realy itchy but it got better when mum put some calamity lotion on it.

When you cut yourslef you have to keep it clean otherwise you might get an infraction.

Dad's arm is hurting. The docter says its tennis elbow but he doesn't play tennis.

I had a visit to the dentist and after that I went in another place to see the high genie

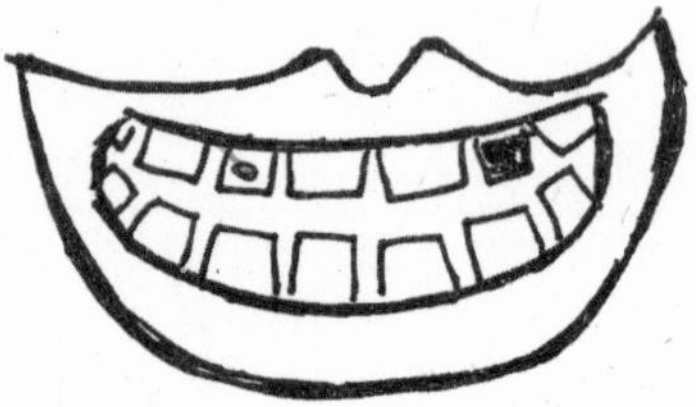

If you have got an alergy like hay fever you can take anti history to make you feel better

My gran has lots of marks on her legs. She says they are called very close vanes.

Laringitus is a really bad cough and you have to take alot of Medicine until you are not hores

HOME TIME

when I cycle home
from school in winter
my mum makes me
wear a high fizzability
jacket.

I hepled my dad in the garage.
He let me
hit some nails
with his hamster.

I love watching the adverts on telly. My favourite is the one with the Durex doggy.

For my party we went to the blowing alley. When we had been blowing we went for a drinck and a buger.

At brownies this week
we lernt to do sin language.

Tow times a week we have a nashonal
tottery. There are six balls and a
boneless ball.

...and then Mr. Browning showed us how climbers use tampons to grip on to their roc.

I learnt fensing. Fensing is when you fight with a sod.

I go to St Johns to lern fist aid. I have lernt how to do a bondage and I got to practice on Mr Terry. He is the leader.

I take the dog for a walk in the pork every evening.

The girl who collects our rent has stopped coming. Now we have a rent boy instead.

My tummy rambles after school so I have chocolet suggestures when I get home.

I saw some grillers at the zoo, they werr big and herry like my dad.

My mum saw my messy bedroom and said it was abdominal I felt a lot of guilt.

Wen my dog wants to go outside he bakes a lot.

My mum told me that my bed shits wont lay themselfs.

My dad luvs watching the footy.– he says it's poultry in motion.

I usea to not like our pet dog because he was viscose. he has groaned on me now

Dad toked about weapons of mass digestion while eating dinner. I'm worried about this. I dont want to get bumbed.

We had a swimming pull dug in our garden and my dad filled it with his big nose.

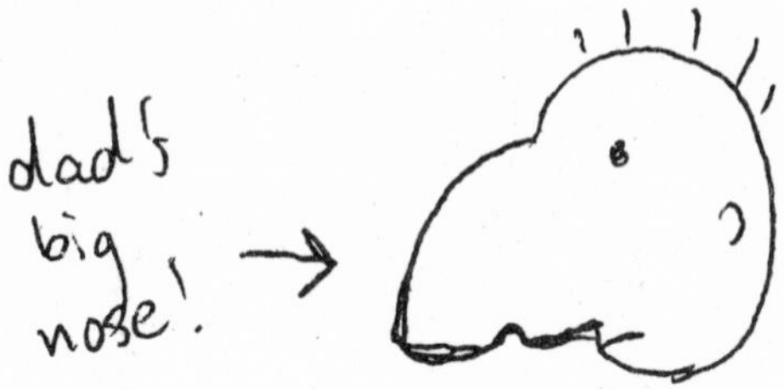

If my parents think Im good I get some sweats.

My frend invited me to see
his hoes on Saturday.

My mum keeps ghosts in our garden,
they keep nippling the washing

I had spots last night. Mum said it was heat radish.

When I was naughty mum made me stand in the corner to make an egs sample of me.

Daddy was quiet this morning so I asked him for a penny for his socks.

The big boys ride home on the top dick of the bus

I love going to the cinema and having cop porn.

Dad came home with a big metal bin. He is going to insinuate old papers in it.

Mum taked me, dannyand peter to the bowling alley. Im not very good at bo ling.

Mummy had a cry today. I think She might be teething like baby jesus.

i went to the shops to get new trainors and they gave me a bigger sighs.

The car trip was long and boring. We drived along time on motorways and jewel carriageways.

When we go to the Shopping centre I like going up and down the excavator.

it was rayning on the walk home and I jumped on loads of muddy poodles.

I love my gloves. They are stripy and shaped like my hand

We had a football match after school. I scored a goat and my teem one.

I couldnt go home because I got a detenshon Mr. Saunders said me and james were a couple of scaly wigs.

It was really hot weather on Sunday so I sat in the paddling poo.

Dad went to the garage to
fill up and let me put
the disease in the car.

Mum and dad had a
man here to do
measuring. He is going
to build a wooden
dick in the garden.

I went to the shops
with mum and dad
stayed at home to
watch the hearse
racing.

Dad said he couldn't here
himself think so he pressed
the newt button on the
TV remote

FRIENDS AND FAMILY

My grandad has got
a large organ. He
says one day he will
give it to me but I
have to lern how to
play it.

This wikend we went shopping.
I got some new shoes and
mummy got a new pair of
tits.

My mum is a barista which means she is always going to court.

When it is my birthday dad said I could have a whore cake all to myself.

When I go to nanas house she bakes lots of cakes and my favourite are hot cross bums.

When I was foul, I had a speshul party and a cak which I shared with all my firends.

Mum and dad were panting in my bedroom this weekend.

Mummy had been in the bath and when she dryed her hair she saw her bush was missing. We all looked for it but daddy let her have his coam.

I have lots of fiends at school and I have even more fiends at home.

...and I took a bunch of violents home for my mum...

We have found out that my anty Mary is stagnant and she will be having a baby in March.

The funny thing about my family is that they are all divers. My uncle Tim is a taxi diver, my uncle Steve is a bus diver and my dad is a van driver.

Me and Simon are best friends. We love to play with each other and we do it all the time.

My mum goes to jim every firday. She always comes home too tired to do anything.

We took my baby sister to the panto for the first time this year. We went to see Sleeping Beauty.

Every time we go
Shopping we have the
same fuss. Dad wants
to read the Mirror but
mum wants her Daily
Male.

We went to visit my dad's boss this
holiday. He lives in a big hose.

We are taking my little sister to see Satan this weekend.

On Sunday my dad filmed me falling intoour pond by axident. We are going to send it to Youive Been Farmed.

My uncle is impotent. He is the boss of a big factory

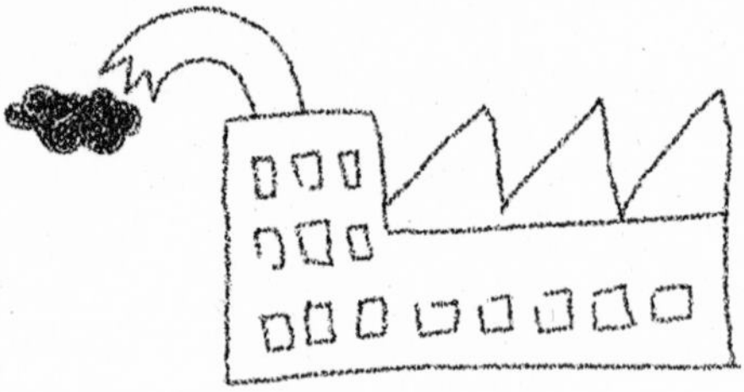

My mum writes the chek out and my dad looks at it and sins.

It was a disaster at the weekend. Granddad's pet bog, Sooki, ran off and we lost her. We asked everybody have you seen a brun and white bog but they didn't have. We was going to ring the bogs home but she came back.

MY DAD LOOKS FUNNY. HE HAS GROAN A BREAD. HE HAD A MUST DASH BEFOR BUT I THINK HIS BREAD LOOKS SILLY.

My grandad yoused to be a cool Miner wen he was yung.

My uncle had to wipe the widows with a wet cloth yestday because the rain made them derty.

Dad was working in the garden and he ascked mum if she could come and give him a hard. She was bisy so Aunty Jo went instead.

My mum was a bit shook up yesterday because she had a dump in the car.

My mum has to go to a fizzy therapist every week.

My gran has a huge chest. We keep our toys in it.

Aunt Claire and uncle Keeth ride a tamtrum bicycle everywhere.

My dad has got a new Car. It is a Raver.

My uncle Jake died last week and he still isn't better.

Grandad won't let me have his old programmes because he wants to keep them for his posterior.

My favourite dog is
a cocky spaniard.

My family believe in star
signs I am Virgo, Billy is Taurus
and mum is the rum.

Bens mum says Im a bad effluence on him.

We wet on dads frends boat. He left off a distrust flair. It was super cool.

My grandad doesn't have any hair so he is bold.

Mum was scarred of the super big spider. Dad said she was a cowherd.

Uncle Billy and Auntie Joan rent a flat but there living with us soon cos there tenacity has stopped.

Nanny was happy because she won money on a Scratch card. Now she will celibate with a party.

My grandma is a very nice lady but her skin doesn't fit her face.

Nan can't walk very much now so she has got a mobility scooter to help her get to the shops

When mums cross with dad she says
she rude the day she met him

My friend Sally lives
in New York now. She
gets dollars and
sense for pocket money.

My baby brother
learns frenetic
sounds at nursery
to help him speak.

Karen was nervous about her exam results. Dad said him and mum were on ten hooks.

We are lerning all about our ancestry with a family three. It's called geniality.

my birfday party was at bugger king. All my friends had beef buggers and cheeps.

All the people in our family went to baby ellies cristening. Last week another baby we know got capsized.

My mum tort me to always write fack you notes for my present. I'm good at saying fack you.

Dad's best frend rich is getting marred soon so he is going on the slag do

I liked the food alan and sues wedding inception. There was a disk cow afterwoods but I was in bed.

we were playing in bens mums office on the computer, I was tolled off when I broke the moose

Daddy likes to go jogging. I don't like jogging because it makes daddy's face leak.

Jenny has a big trampoline in the garden. We jumped on it for ages and got really high.

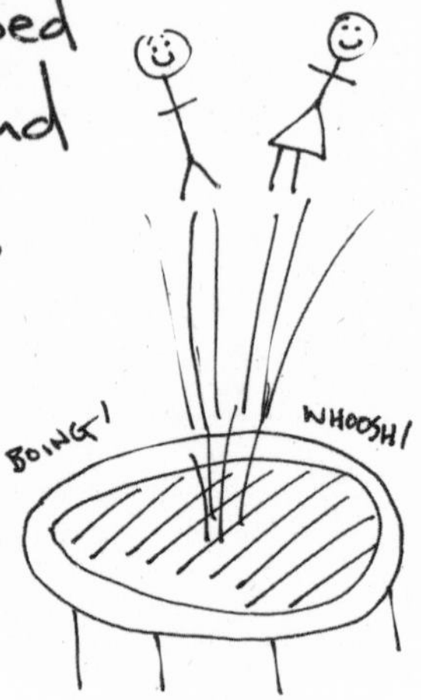

We went to see my cussons on new years eaf. We wished them all happy new ears.

I like bank hollidays because dad is at home. He works nights but not on bank days.

I love sprinklers on my ice cream. Yum yum.

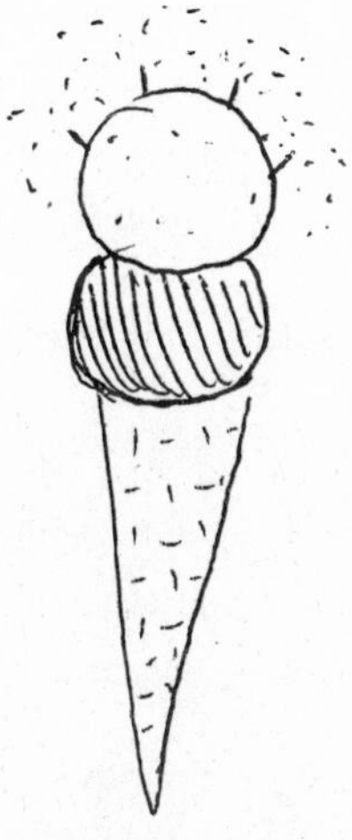

WHEN I GROW UP

I Like sewing. I would Like to be a sewer when I grow up.

When I grow up I want to learn how to tipe quickly and I want to be a tipissed

I would like to be a signtist and I would like to work in a lavatory.

My uncle shouts at my cousins and mocks them do chores. One day they are going to be policemen and policewomen so they can put him in prison.

I wuld like to be a vet becouse I enjoy meating animals.

My sister is a babyseller. She gets money from the grown ups, and she sells their babys while they are away. I would like to be a babyseller too.

My dad wants me to be a nurse but I want to be a dancer. But I can do both. Work in the day time and a dancer in the night time. He says this could be true because he once saw of ladys who did that.

My friends think I shud be a comeddien when I grow up becos I am fanny and it maks them larf.

I am going to be a scientogolist because I am cleaver at science.

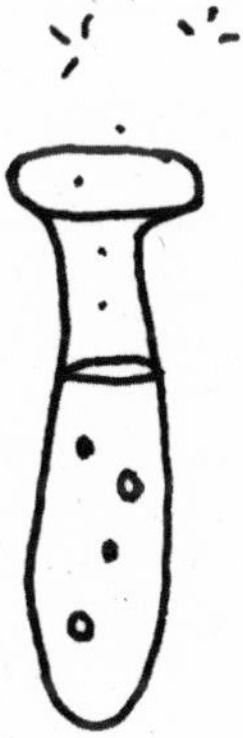

When I get older I want to work with monkeys. My favourite monkeys are chumps and orange tangs.

When I get big I want to reech the
Sealing like my really big brother can do

I want to ren away to the circus and do
tricks like being a jugular and do the
trapease

I'm not sure if I want to grow up.
Will my bones fall out like my teeth,
so that bigger ones can grow?x

My dad is a postman and so was granddad.
I would like to be a postman and deliver all the males.

I'm going to work in
a skycrapper and
ern lots of money.

When I grow up I'm going
to shave my arm pips

I want to be a toucher when I am bigger like Mr. Fox and Miss Andrews.

When I'm older I want to learn to drive a cat.

I would love to have lots of babys when I'm a grownup. My mummy says I have to wait until I'm much older but tina across our road has lots of babys and she isn't grownup. She also has lots of husbends.

GRANPA STEVE WAS BUTCH.
I LIKE EATING MEET SO BEING A BUTCH MIGHT BE A GOOD JOB.

I want to be in the oil limpet games and try ruining races.

I want to be a baker becos if you are a baker you need bread a lot. It feels nice.

I have a super cool toothbrush. Its eclectic and its really powerful.

I am helping my mum to make a pachwork kilt.

When I am a big girl I want
to wear lapstick like my mummy.

I just want to watch tv
and eat chirps all day

lots & lots & lots
of
Chirps!

If I can be a astronought I will fly in a pocket to see if there is cheese on the Moon.

I want to be an anterior desiner. I will change all the things in people's houses and desine them so they look nice.

I write stories the best at school so I could write books maybe when I'm older. I think I might be a friction writer.

I will be a painter and dickerator like my dad and uncle.

My friends dad is a flight amendment. He has looks after everybody on the plane.

I want to be a kernel in the army. They get lots of badges to wear

I want a bee and bee and have lots of gussets to stay.

I dont no what to do. Iam going to the career office at school to see if they have a vice for me.

I want to be a teacher because they have really long Holydays like me.

I will manger peoples money. That's called a cuntant

I want to be a waiter in a restraint. If people like the food they will give me trips.

BEDTIME

I will go to another country and be a pear which means I will look after children and do the cooking

Sam's mum looked at her little boy. 'Come on, it's up to the land of nob for you' she said.

My little sister still has
to sleep with the
light on because she
is afraid of the dark.

My dad works nights so he
spends all day in deb.

Befor I go to bed I
Sometimes have a mug
of warm milk to help
me go to sleep. Mummy
has a mug of wine.

My baby bother sleeps in a cat in my bedroom.

It is verry noisy at night for me because we live above a pube

... and suddenly the door opened and banged against the wall. I felt a lamp in my throat.

I sleep in my bedroom. My broter sleeps in his bedrom. My mummy sleeps in hers and daddys bedrom but daddy sumtimes sleeps on the sofa with our dog. I think this is because he grawls like a dog when he is snooring in his sleep.

My sister is 3. When she goes to bed she calls her blanket a wanket. It makes my mum and big sister larf.

Dad works at night times so he sumtimes has forty wanks in the day.

I had a scary bad dreem but it wasn't reel. It was just a pigment of my imagination.

I hate washing my hair
because the poo shem
gets in my eyes and stings.

I don't like nightmares. I like having
Sweat dreams.

Mum always pores
me a drink of
nice worm milk
before I go to bed.

baby harry sleeps in his
cot and mum and dad
have a baby motor so
they can here what
hes doing.

When I cant sleep at night my mum says I should try to count ship.

Me and timmy share a bonk bed. He has the top bonk and I have the bottom bonk.

Baby Amy keeps
crying at nite. Mum
and dad says she needs
to have a proper
bedtime rude teen.

I spin the mubile above the
babys cot. It helps him
sleep.

Some times my mum lets me piss
my baby brother in his pisschair
if I is careful

I go to bed at 7. Then I can
hear mummy and daddy
watching all the soups on
TV downstairs.

it was so hot in my room in august. I had a van in my room to keep me cool.

some times when it is hot in summer we camp in the garden and sleep under the stairs.

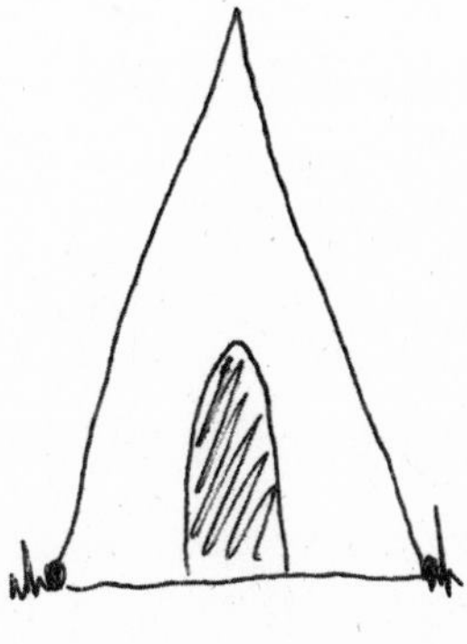

When I go to seep
overs at my frends
house I take a
Seeping bag to seep in.

mum put my tooth under
the pillow and in the
morning the tooth ferry
had given me a 50 pee.

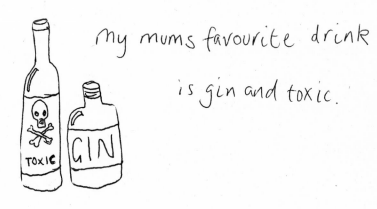

My mums favourite drink

is gin and toxic.

I was tired all day. I didn't sleep well.
Mum said I was tossing all nite.

when I get tucked in dad turns off the lights and says dont let the big beds bite.

I have a humiliator in the room sometimes becos it makes me breeth better

Mummy told me she is fragrant.
I hope I get a sister.

Uncle Derek doesn't sleep
at night because he
has somalia.

I like mummy and daddy's matress becos its ~~soft~~ and skwishy. They say it is made from mammary foam.

I put my clothes away at bed time. I put my trousers in the drawer and I hang up my school shit.

When my socks get wet in puddles
I put them on the raidy heater
in my bedroom.

Jamie has a weird
bed. Its a matress
on the floor and its
called a crouton.

baby alexander keeps getting over tired but mummy hopes its just a faze.

my mums car broke down and my dad says its because she needs a new crotch.

my gran loves gardening except
when she has to pull pricks out of
her hands from the roses

My dad says I should drink a
glass of muck everyday to help
my boner grow strong.

our neighbour gets cross when
my football goes in his garden but
he does kick my balls back for me.

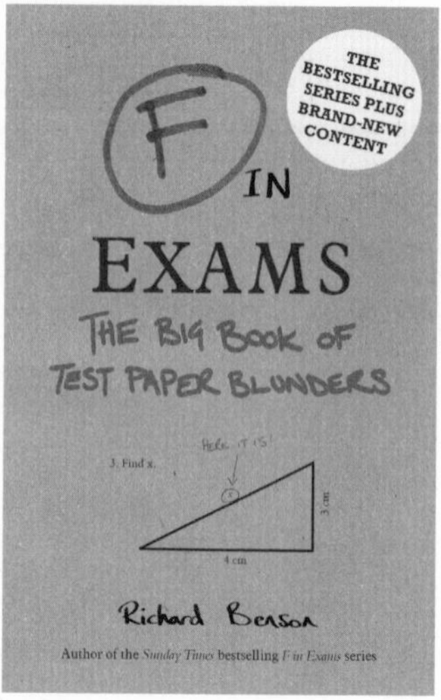

F IN EXAMS

The Big Book of
Test Paper Blunders

Richard Benson

£9.99

Hardback

ISBN:978-1-84953-924-1

Exams have never been so hilarious!

Banish the horror of school days with this bumper edition of the world's ~~worst~~ best test paper blunders. Bursting with misunderstandings, misspellings and spirited – if ultimately incorrect – answers, this collection brings together the most head-scratching, side-splitting examples from the *F in Exams* series.